Raising Your Child & Yourself:

A No Nonsense Guide for Young Single Parents

By: LaKeisha Giles

Raising Your Child & Yourself

Published Work © 2006 by LaKeisha Giles

All rights reserved. No part of this book shall be reproduced, stored in a retrieval system, or transmitted by any means, electronic, mechanical, photocopying, recording, or otherwise, without written permission from the publisher. No patent liability is assumed with respect to the use of the information contained herein. Although every precaution has been taken in the preparation of this book, the publisher and author assume no responsibility for errors or omissions. Neither is any liability assumed for damages resulting from the use of the information contained herein.

International Standard Book Number: 978-0-6152-1211-1

Library of Congress Catalog Card Number:

Printed in the United States of America

First Printing: December 2006

Trademarks

TABLE OF CONTENTS

INTRODUCTION 6-7

PART 1: LEARN SOMETHING ABOUT SOMETHING 10-21
  1. Why Pursue Higher Education? 12-13
  2. What type of school should you attend? 13-15
  3. How should you choose your new career? 15-17
  4. How can I pay for college? 17-18
  5. Where does my child go while I am in Class? 19
  6. Soak up the Knowledge 19-21

PART II: NEED MONEY? HERE'S HOW TO GET IT! 22-35
  7. Mistakes to Avoid 24-28
  8. Saving and Investing 28-32
  9. Ways to Make Extra Money 32-35

PART III: MANAGING YOUR RELATIONSHIPS 36-47
  10. Why Is This So Important? 38-39
  11. Relationships with Significant Others 39-41
  13. Relationships with Your Children 41-43

14. Relationship With Yourself 44-47

PART IV: YOUR SPIRITUALITY 48-61
15. Getting Started 50-58
16. Change Your Life 58-59
17. Talk About God 59-61

CONCLUSIONS 62-63

APPENDIX 64-68

ABOUT THE AUTHOR 70

DEDICATIONS:

This book is dedicated to my 2 wonderful children, Khayla & Davian, who taught me 99% of what I discuss in this book and encouraged me to learn the rest.

Special thanks to Henry & Charlotte Giles, Emily Perry, Tiffany Washington, & "Cup" because without you I would not have made it this far.

In loving memory of Jennie Hawthorne & Mamie Johnson

Raising Your Child & Yourself

INTRODUCTION

In our ever-changing world, few things remain constant. Technology is relentlessly changing, as well as the environment, politics, music, and every other facet of life. The family structure is one entity that has been literally redefined. Two-parent households are rapidly becoming the minority because single parents are commandeering more and more households; more specifically young single mothers. The effect of this influx of adolescent parents has created an entire generation of parents that are not yet mature, stable, or self sufficient. Although the problems that are arising because of this growing statistic are becoming more and more prevalent, their needs and issues are not being addressed; in fact they are often over looked or simply ignored.

This oversight occurs for many reasons. One reason is that single mothers are often reproached rather than admired. Many feel that rather than being victims, these women are in unfortunate positions upon their own accord because they are unwed mothers, divorcees, and widowers. At times these families are even viewed as liabilities. This group of women is often uneducated, or less educated, and therefore dependent on public assistance for survival. Less educated individuals tend historically not to vote, thus leaving their issues further out in the cold.

What knowledge and skills do I have that give me the authority to teach others? I am simply a woman that became a single mother at a young age. I learned a lot through my journey and often wished that there were more tools and resources out there to help and guide me. Many magazines and books gave advice on the steps to becoming financially stable, managing relationships, or furthering education, but none of them were tailored specifically to me and my situation. Also, a lot of these resources tell you what you should do, but not how it can be done. For example, they tell us to further our education, but how do you do that on one income with children?

People desert their dreams and run from impediments too often in life because of the way that we view them. We tend to look at issues holistically, and that holistic view is often big and scary. The thought of trying to solve a large problem is often enough to stop you from taking action to solve it. But, when you break the problem down into tiny pieces and solve the tiny issues one by one, you suddenly begin to see what once seemed daunting and impossible as something that is manageable and not insurmountable. The key to being a success is learning how to attack your problem.

In this book, I attempt to provide this information, not from a professional view, but from a personal one. I would love for other single parents to learn from my mistakes and successes. This book will benefit younger single mothers the most, but all single parents will find it beneficial. Hopefully this resource will provide an outlet or resource tool to make the journey that you are beginning less frightening. Buy it for yourself or give it to your daughters, granddaughters, nieces, etc. Help them to become proactive in their fight for survival.

I encourage you to write in this book, highlight important text, and personalize the steps to fit your needs and desires. Sometimes seeing information in writing can open your eyes and encourage you to keep trying and moving forward.

Before you begin reading, take the time right now to write down your three best qualities. Think about your answer before you write it, and be specific. Earmark this page because we will come back to these qualities later on in this book.

My three best qualities are:

1. _____

2. _____

3. _____

PART I. LEARN SOMETHING ABOUT SOMETHING

1. Why Pursue Higher Education?

In recent years pursuance of higher education has transitioned from being an option to becoming a necessity. Jobs that once required high school diplomas now require college degrees. Degreed positions now go to master's degreed candidates. Workers that have no high school diploma or G.E.D. are increasingly being forced to accept menial jobs, if they can find one at all. This fact leads me to stress the importance of higher education. This should be one of the primary focuses of a single parent because of the following reasons:

1. **More options.** The more education that you have, the more employment options you will have.
2. **Stronger work history.** The more employment options you have the better chance for you to build a solid and well-rounded work history.

3. **Chances for Advancement.** The more dimensional your work history is, the better your chances for advancement in your job.
4. **Pass it on.** The more education that you have, the more you can teach your child.

2. What type of school should you attend?

If you have not already done so, the first step that must be taken is the completion of your high school diploma or GED. Most community colleges offer basic education classes, sometimes at no cost. Area churches and libraries may also offer classes or tutoring. Take advantage of these classes and get your diploma so that you can focus on choosing a career.

Your education should not stop at the high school level. Take the initiative to pursue higher education, which comes in many different forms. Four-year degrees are almost synonymous with the word college, but for single parents this may not be an option. This does not mean that a single parent cannot go back to school. There are other options:

1. 4-Year degree programs
2. 2-year degree programs
3. 1-year certification programs
4. Trade Schools
5. Jr. Colleges

6. Online degrees
7. Tutors
8. Friends and family members.

Use the space provided below to list your top two options for furthering your education. Also list a school in your area with this classification. After you write down your answers, go online and request information from these schools. There is no cost associated with requesting information!

My educational options are:

1. Type of degree: _____
   School / College: _____
   Website: _____

2. Type of degree: _____
   School / College: _____
   Website: _____

Whatever career or college you choose, your main focus should be on choosing a career that suits you and your situation. Take your education seriously and attend classes regularly. What may seem like a huge sacrifice now will pay dividends in the end if you maintain your focus on the goals that you have set for yourself. The earlier that you take the initiative to pursue your education, the better off you will be.

Working, raising a child, and going to school was one of the hardest things that I ever did, but it was also the smartest. Many parents want to ignore the fact that the instant that they became single parents, no matter what the reason, their lives instantly became harder. There are two ways that a person can choose to deal with obstacles: complain about them, or roll up your sleeves and move them out of the way.

3. How should you choose your new career?

The first and most critical step in going back to school is choosing an area of interest. Two things need to be taken into account: the job market in your area and your personal interests. Notice that I mentioned job market first. Single parents are forced to support entire households single-handedly. The need to be extremely marketable is paramount in order to do this.

Personally, I made the mistake of ignoring the most lucrative job market in my area. Like most of the country, the major industry that is actively hiring and actually experiencing shortages is the healthcare industry. Nurses, CNA's, doctors, pharmacists, and dental associates are in extremely high demand. If I had chosen this field, I would have had more jobs and positions to choose from. Even though this industry is not my particular interest, the opportunities that it presents are strong enough that this deserved consideration.

Take the time to look at the career section of your city's newspaper on a Sunday evening. Take note of the fields that have the most opportunities available, then research the three that interest you most. Determine the amount of education that is required for the position, the entry level and median pay for the field, and companies in your area that offer positions in this field.

Get your local newspaper. On the left, list the 5 careers fields with the most job offerings (Ex. Medical, Administrative, etc.). On the right, list the three that interest you the most.

Top Career Fields
1. _____
2. _____
3. _____
4. _____
5. _____

My Career Fields
1. _____
2. _____
3. _____

Research your career fields by using the Internet, library, and people that you may know in the field. Do the three qualities that you listed about your self on page 8 fit with the job descriptions and responsibilities of your chosen field? If not, should you rethink your career field? What amount of education do you need for this field? Do your college choices on page 14 offer the degree associated with your career choice?

Another factor that you should consider is whether or not the school that you are choosing caters to adult learners. Many schools now offer night, online, and weekend classes to fit the schedules of working adults. This may be the ultimate determining factor when you decide which college is right for you. It is important to thoroughly do your research before you make any decisions. You do not have money to waste on applying to schools that do not fit your needs.

4. How can I pay for college?

The next major decision involved in going back to school is determining how your education will be financed. It is critical that the decision to return to school is made sooner rather than later because younger adults in general have fewer bills weighing them down. There are a variety of options available to you if you want to go back to school:

1. Student loans
2. Grants
3. Scholarships
4. Family and friends
5. Tuition reimbursement from your present employer.

There are many programs and grants that are catered towards adults that are going back to school to further their education. Finding them simply takes a little research. All college websites have links for financial assistance and scholarships. There are even grants that will pay for your college application fee. I should warn you that most of the chapters in this book refer back to this one, because I feel that it is so important. You will have trouble following the other steps in the book if you do not take on this task first. Do not make excuses and say that it is too hard. Choosing not to further your education is a harder and longer road to journey than most young people realize.

Use the Internet or library and write down three scholarships that you qualify for and their websites. Go ahead and request more information or print the instructions. Again, this will not cost you anything.

My scholarships / grants:
1. Scholarship: _____
    Website: _____

2. Scholarship: _____
    Website: _____

3. Scholarship: _____
    Website: _____

5. Where does my child go while I am in Class?

Many colleges offer family housing, but if you are not staying on campus or if you are not attending a four year program then other options must be pursued. Childcare options for parents that are attending school are out there, but your options mainly depend on whether you are attending college full time (12 or more semester hours) or part time (6 hours or less). Here are a few places that you can look:

1. **Government Agencies.** There are Government programs out there aimed at parents that are returning to school. Many times they will help pay for childcare if you are enrolled in school at least part-time. Contact your local Social Services Department and Child Care Resources for more information.
2. **Classmates**. College students are often in need of extra money. One semester I had an evening class. I paid one of my classmates that I trusted a few dollars to watch my daughter while I was in class. It did not cost me much, she made extra money, and I did not have far to go to drop my daughter off.
3. **Friends and Family**. Many times friends and family members will watch your child for free (especially in the evening). Sometimes all you have to do is ask and plan in advance.

6. Soak up the Knowledge

Remember that education comes in many different forms, not just in a textbook. It is important that you have knowledge to pass on to your child. Children learn best by example, so if they see that you are constantly reading and learning they will want to do the same. Here are some places that you can educate yourself for little or no cost:

1. Read the newspaper daily.
2. Visit the library and pick up some non-fiction reading such as a biography.
3. Read magazines that focus on various subjects such as Parenting Magazine, Black Enterprise or Time Magazine.
4. Watch the news.
5. Watch educational channels such as National Geographic or Discovery Health.
6. Attend seminars, workshops, or free classes offered in your area.
7. Browse the Internet.
8. Join a book club or a civic group and learn more about your community.

Name 3 educational magazines, seminars, or clubs that you are interested in.

My interests:
    1. _____
    2. _____
    3. _____

It is important to remember that if you do not want to improve your situation and fight for something more, no one else will either. Chances are, if you are a young parent you are not prepared in any way to raise your child - yet. Care enough about both of your futures to take the time, energy, and courage to improve your situation.

PART II. NEED MONEY?

HERE'S HOW TO GET IT!

7. Mistakes to Avoid

I made many mistakes when it came to my finances that I would love to prevent other single parents from making. I made my mistakes because of a lack of knowledge in some instances, and a lack of planning in others. This part of the book focuses on using the resources that you have and making them work for you.

1. **Student Loans:** It may seem peculiar that I encourage college education by any means, including student loans, but now I am going to tell you to beware. Not really beware, but be aware. When I was in college and received my refund checks from my student loans they helped me tremendously. I bought textbooks, paid a few outstanding bills, and spent a little on myself. Just remember, you have to pay this money back plus interest for unsubsidized loans! For this reason, I encourage you to only borrow what you need. When it is

time to pay back the loans research interest rates and consolidation of your loans (if you have more than one).

Also, be sure to pay your loan payments on time. Missing student loan payments can really hurt your credit, and even if you file bankruptcy, you still have to pay these loans back! They can, and will garnish your wages, snatch your income tax refunds, etc. Talk to your lenders because they are very understanding and will work with you when it comes to paying your loan back if you communicate with them.

2. **Car payments, credit cards, high speed Internet, etc:** Just say no. You are a single parent. You cannot afford an expensive car payment, 5 high interest credit cards, and an extreme cable bill. A first class, modern car would be nice. Do not do it. When you buy a new car, consider the fact that not only are the car payments higher on a newer car, but so is the maintenance, taxes, and car insurance. Also remember that SUV's and vans use almost twice as much gas as smaller cars. These little incidentals add up quickly.

Credit cards have become a necessary evil. You need them to establish credit, and you need them for emergencies. The problem is that people do not reserve their use for these two things. A single parent should. Interest rates on credit cards that are not fully paid monthly are tremendous. If you can resist the temptation of charging items, then get two cards and let them collect dust in your wallet. If not, then avoid them.

The cash advance, or salary advance industry is being attacked in most states for many valid reasons, but until it is more heavily regulated avoid them. This is a hole that many people fall into and can not climb out of. Do some research and find another way. Some banks and credit unions offer similar services at much more reasonable rates. Do not just give people your money for a quick fix.

3. **Entertainment & Luxury expenses:** Cross all of the following entertainment expenses off of monthly expenditure list:

- Hairdresser
- Nail salon
- Movies & Clubs
- Cigarettes & alcohol
- Cable TV with premium channels
- Video systems & games
- Name brand shoes & clothing
- Jewelry
- Expensive vacations & trips
- Lottery tickets

I am not saying that you can never have these things, but you can save a tremendous amount of money if you cut down on, or entirely eliminate these activities. The money that is wasted on these items could pay for the tuition that you can not afford or the savings that you swore you could not generate. Be smarter with your money.

4. **Cut back on eating out.** Eating out daily is costly. If you eat out for breakfast and lunch each day, you are tossing away money

that could be used in a more productive way. Try carrying your lunch from home at least three days a week. Instead of packing your kids' lunches, let them eat the lunch at school. School lunches are inexpensive and well rounded. The children of single parents often qualify for reduced or free lunches. Do not waste your money on costly prepackaged lunches!

5. **Lower your gas costs.** With the steadily rising cost of gas, conservation is a must. Do not make unnecessary trips. Plan your routes in advance and keep your vehicle well maintained. A car that has properly inflated tires, up to date tune-ups and oil changes, and clean air filters will burn less gas. Maintenancing a car can be difficult for a person with a limited income, but it will save money in the end. Another consideration is, if it is available, using public transportation or car-pooling. Many cities have reasonable fares for bus rides. Take advantage of it!

List 2 major strategies that you can implement immediately to begin reducing your expenses. What can you cut back on?

I can reduce my expenses by:

1. _____
   _____

2. _____
   _____

There are many other areas that could be addressed in this section, such as cell phone and pet bills, but the main key to all of these tips and ideas is not to overextend yourself. Rent or mortgage, car payments and insurance, childcare, utilities, etc can and will bog you down. Avoid adding unnecessary expenses. Also, become aware of services in your area that can help you. Do not suffer in silence. Research childcare assistance options, WIC, etc. These programs are there to help you, do not be too proud to use them.

8. Saving and Investing

Saving money is easier than it sounds. The problem for me is not sitting some money aside each month from my check. My problem is not dipping into that money by the end of the month! The important thing to remember is that there are different ways that you can save money. Here are a few saving and investing tips to get you started:

1. **Take a class**. A professor once told me that every adult should take a finance class, even if it has nothing to do with their career goals. I believe that he was right. A finance or entry level accounting class can teach you how to balance your checkbook, create a budget, invest, and so much more. Learning how to manage your money early can save you time and money later in your life.

2. **Protect Your Credit Rating**. Many adults learn the hard way that your credit rating is extremely important. Many times comedians joke about how bad their credit is, but trust me, bad credit

is not a laughing matter! Banks, car dealers, renters, and even employers use your credit report to make decisions about you. Take the initiative as a young adult to build your credit and to maintain it. Pay your bills on time and monitor your credit often by requesting copies of your credit report from the three major credit bureaus (Equifax, Experian and TransUnion).

3. **Child support.** If you do not have a child support order in place for your child, it is your duty to pursue one. Many women make the mistake of either not filing for child support, or not keeping up with the status of their case once it is filed.

4. **Pay your self first.** This is not a new concept, but it is one that is often ignored. If you can pay your bills and your hairstylist and go out to eat, then you can put some money into savings. A savings account that you put only $25 per month in turns into $300 plus interest at the end of a year. Increase your monthly amount and watch your savings grow. If your car breaks down, or your child suddenly gets sick, or the air conditioner goes out in the middle of the summer, have something to fall back on!

I recently learned that I needed 2 savings accounts, one that I do not touch, and one that I can dip into. You should set aside money each month that you do not touch. Also, open savings accounts for your children. This can be the beginning of their college funds, or accounts that they save money in when they begin working. Even if you only put a couple of dollars a pay period into their accounts, this money will gain interest and mature over time. Another tip is, if you are receiving child support put a portion of your child support payments into their personal savings accounts.

5. **Take advantage of your 401K**. Many full time jobs offer 401K to their employees. Take full advantage of it. Make the maximum that your company will match your minimum. If do not understand what it is or how it works, educate yourself. Not taking advantage of this is like giving money away.

6. **Get Insurance.** Car insurance, health insurance, homeowners or renters insurance are necessary. Do not risk being caught without them. When we look for areas to cut costs, this should not be one of them. The end result of not having it will be the most costly.

7. **Become a bargain shopper.** If you have a cash flow problem and are not taking the time to shop around for the best price, you are wasting money. If you do not have a car or the time to drive to different stores for the best price, use the Internet. Most retailers have online stores. Use these websites to find the best prices. Do not forget to clip coupons and scour the sales paper for the best deals. Saving $5 here and $10 there can easily add up to $50 in a month.

8. **Buy in bulk**. Buying what you know you will need in bulk can save you a lot of money over time. Get a membership in a wholesale warehouse such as Sam's Club or Costco and stock up! Paper towels, toilet tissue, soap, laundry detergent, and canned foods are nonperishable items that are must haves and can be bought at cheaper prices in bulk and then stored. There are many warehouses

that sell meat and frozen foods in bulk. A good time to stock up on these items is during tax time. Instead of splurging your income tax return, save most of it, pay off some bills, and then buy a few items that you will need in bulk.

9. **Loose Change**. It may not seem possible, but nickels, dimes, and pennies really do add up. Every time you are given change back after a cash transaction, put the change in a piggy bank. One year I actually bought all of my Christmas presents from change that I saved for a year! Some banks, such as Bank of America, offer programs that will transfer the change from a debit account into a savings account. This money can really come in handy for lunch, gas, or other incidentals that pop up. Encouraging your children to do the same can teach them how to save as well.

10. **Take care of what you have**. If it ain't broke, you don't have to fix it! Learn to care for the items that you already have, whether it is learning how to properly wash your clothes, or how to use your garbage disposal so that it does not get clogged. Read the instructions for your DVD player, get the oil changed in your car, show your children how to clean and take care of their shoes and clothes. Do not create unnecessary bills for yourself if it can be avoided!

11. **Keep your receipts.** You never know when you may need a receipt. Whether it is for tax purposes or for the return of an item, keep your receipts for at least two years. Unless you have taken finance classes, you never know what may end up being a tax

deduction. Text books, gas, moving expenses, and many other things can often become important, so make a receipts folder or drawer in your house and throw them in there.

List the 4 ways that you can begin saving money today.

I can save money by:
1. _____
_____
2. _____
_____
3. _____
_____
4. _____
_____

9. Ways to Make Extra Money

One way of staying afloat as a single parent is by becoming a financial magician. You take too little money and make it appear as if it is a lot of money. One way that you can do less magic and have more money in reality is by finding a way to make extra money. Every single parent needs a hustle. Here are some ways that you can bring extra money into your household:

1. **Part time job.** This is the most common way of making extra money, but it is not always the best option for single parents. Finding a part time job also means finding and paying for a part time babysitter. If you are blessed enough to have free babysitters and the time to work an extra job, then you must get another job. Even if it is not for long you can put this money away for savings or use it to pay for your insurance and college costs.

2. **Turn your hobby into extra cash.** In college, I typed 70+ wpm and had a knack for writing. I used those talents to type and proof essays and papers for other students for a small fee. When you are in college or are a college graduate, neighboring parents are willing to pay serious money to get tutors for their children – often up to $20 per hour!

Use your talents and abilities. Somebody will pay you for them.

- If you can draw, sell your artwork, or do portraits.
- If you can sing or play an instrument, give lessons or play on Sunday mornings for a local church.
- If you have technical skills, older adults will pay you to learn computer skills.
- Create websites and newsletters.
- If you can sew or crochet, make clothing.
- Cut your neighbors grass.
- Clean houses in your neighborhood.
- Can you cook? Start your own catering service.

- Are you handy with tools? Do handy work around your neighborhood.
- Do you do taxes? Keep abreast of the tax laws and do your family member's yearly tax returns for a small fee.
- Wash cars? Start your own detailing service.
- Are you a whiz when it comes to cleanliness? Start your own housekeeping service.

If you do not have a talent, but do have interests, refer back to chapter 1 and pursue taking classes. (Taking classes or getting certifications may generate more interest in your work.)

List your 3 best talents. How can you make money from this talent?

My money-making talents are:

1. _____
   _____

2. _____
   _____

3. _____
   _____

3. **Use the Internet.** You would be amazed to learn what people will buy online. Sites like Ebay, Overstock.com, and Half.com allow you to sell different items virtually all over the world. Make jewelry, scented candles, pottery, key chains, or dolls and sell your items on Ebay. Sell used clothing, shoes, books, magazines, toys, appliances, movies, and music with a few keystrokes. Clean out your closets and your friends and families closets and set up an online store. It does not cost much and can put extra money in your pocket. Use the money from your initial sales to buy more inventory for your online store.

List 5 items that you can sell online. Go online and find the price that this item last sold for.

Item	**Price**
_____	$ _____
_____	$ _____
_____	$ _____
_____	$ _____
_____	$ _____

This is just a small list of some of the things that you can do for extra money. Be creative. Figure out what you like to do, and then find a way to make it work for you.

PART III. MANAGING YOUR RELATIONSHIPS

10. Why Is This So Important?

Up until this point your children have not been mentioned very often in this book. Although they are the most important factor and the reason for this book, the first couple of chapters were not dedicated to them, yet to self-improvement. Why is this? When you become responsible for another human life, you must first have the tools to carry that responsibility. As a parent, you must improve and better yourself FIRST so that you have something to give others, especially your children. That is why it is so important that parents are ready for the responsibility before it comes. Life does not always follow logic so young single parents have to take on the task of growing up and maturing *as* they raise their children.

When you are a single parent, managing your relationships becomes extremely important. Every relationship that you have affects your child either directly or indirectly. Whether it is your family, friends, coworkers, or significant other, the people that you choose to trust around your children greatly impact them. Above all else, be aware of that fact. This part of the book will focus on only three of these relationships: Relationships with significant others, your children, and yourself.

11. Relationships with Significant Others

Among the most important relationships that you have, your relationship with your boyfriend, girlfriend, or fiancé, is at the top of that list. Significant others can be either positive or negative influences in your life. The important thing to remember is that when it comes to your child, you should make careful decisions. Many single parents feel that they have to find a mate in order to mother or father their child. Some feel that they need a mate because they are lonely, or tired of carrying their heavy load alone. Some feel that they should take the first mate that comes along and is willing to accept their ready-made family because most men will not accept their kids. Others are just content with dating casually because they do not want a serious relationship to affect their children.

We do not need statistics to prove to ourselves that children with both a mother and father function better in society and become more successful. This is not, however, an excuse for becoming involved with a partner because of the financial stability that they may bring to your household. Your child's safety, security, and comfort are more important than any feeling of loneliness, tiredness, or stress that you as an adult may feel. Do not sacrifice your child for your immediate happiness. Take the time to know the people that you bring into your child's life. Do not introduce your child to every person you date. Do not allow various men to spend the night. You may think that your three-year-old daughter does not notice, but trust me, she does. If you do not want your children to repeat the mistakes that you have made, do not show them how to do it.

If you are tired, lonely, or stressed, rather than seeking comfort in another person, seek it in a trusted friend or family member. Go to church (see chapter 14), or join support groups. Support groups can be PTA's, book clubs, sports functions, any place that you can meet people with similar interests. Find yourself, finish your education, and focus on your career. The next man will come along whether you search for him or you let him come to you. Do not settle for finding any available man as your primary goal in life.

List the 3 most important qualities that you desire in a mate.

I want my mate to be:
1. _____
2. _____
3. _____

Compare your answers to the qualities that you listed for yourself on page 8. Are they compatible? Is this really what you need in a mate, or is something missing?

Part of maturing and growing up is learning to depend on yourself for all of your needs, including your emotional needs. It is ok to ask for help, but do not depend on anyone else to supply your basic needs – not the government, not your parents, and not a man. Dependence on other people or vices, such as drugs or alcohol, weakens your ability to make the best decisions for you and your child. Do not take that chance.

If you have gotten to the place in your life where you are financially, emotionally, and spiritually sound, then put yourself in the right places to meet the person that you desire. Determine for yourself what you would like in a mate. Inventory your likes and dislikes. Then join functions and activities that include your interests. Go to church, go to the library, join a bowling league, or the YMCA; whatever interests you take advantage of it, but make sure that you are ready for what you are searching for.

The important thing is to feel good about you before you worry about feeling good about somebody else. Many young women become single mothers because they are searching for something and thought they could find it in sex or in a relationship with a man. Figure out what you were searching for and deal with that issue before you pursue a relationship. It will not be easy and it will not be a fast journey. But taking the long road will sometimes get you a lot farther in the end than short cuts. Most of all, do not settle. Do not be satisfied with good enough. Not when you and your child deserve the best.

12. Relationships with Your Children

It seems that it should be unnecessary to speak to parents about the relationship that they have with their child, but some young adults do not realize that this relationship needs work as well. One of the many disadvantages that a child in a single parent household faces is the fact that they often have only one outlet; one person to turn to. If you are unapproachable, or in a bad mood, who can they turn to? Do not leave the important issues and lessons that your children must deal with to chance. Be their outlet.

Take the time to play with your child. Young children learn best through play. They also use this time to tell you about their day or show you things that they have learned. You can learn the names of their friends, or what they eat for lunch, or who was bullying them in school during a ten-minute play session. It may not sound like a lot, but some kids do not get their parents full attention for even this long.

List 2 thirty minute activities that you can do with your kid(s) this week and MAKE TIME FOR THEM.

This week my kids and I will:

1. _____
   _____
2. _____
   _____

I help my daughter clean up the kitchen, and while we are doing it I ask her about her friends, her teachers, whether or not she is generally happy with her life. At first your child may not feel comfortable talking to you about certain things, but if you open up the lines of communication, they at least have that option.

Discipline is also part of the relationship that you have with your child. Many families struggle with finding appropriate methods of discipline, but the better you know your child, the better you can lead them in the right direction. The younger you begin setting guidelines and boundaries, the easier it will be. Single parents often have to rely on neighbors, friends, or family members when it comes to childcare and after school care. It is still your responsibility to know where your child is, what they are eating, and what they are doing. Routines help children organize themselves and understand what is expected of them. Drop in on your child at school or daycare, schedule a conference with their teacher, and spot-check their homework assignments. Do not wait until your child is in serious trouble in school or at home to try and do something about it. Be proactive.

13. Relationship With Yourself

When I had my daughter at nineteen I carried a lot of guilt, so my main focus was on fixing the issues that I had caused. I was worried about money and my daughter and school, but I left very little time to worry about myself. If you are going to be a great parent, role model, employee, and friend, you have to make sure to take care of yourself.

1.**Forgive yourself.** Guilt is an emotion that can be extremely difficult to deal with, but it can cause tremendous harm if it is not taken care of. Many single parents feel tremendous guilt because their children do not have two active parents in their lives. We sometimes feel guilty because we have to lean on our family members or government agencies for help. Guilt can also be a result of feeling like you are not doing enough for your child. The best way to deal with this guilt is to recognize it, forgive yourself, and move on.

You can not go back and change or fix the situation that you are in, so focus on improving your situation and not repeating past mistakes. Do the best that you can and accept that you cannot and will not be perfect. If you feel guilt from all of the help that you are receiving, giving back is a great way to show your appreciation. You may not have the money to give someone else, but do you have time to read to the kids at your child's school? Do you have gently used clothing that can go to Goodwill? Can you cook dinner once in a while for that family member that has been so helpful? Make the time to say thank you and you will feel deserving of all of the gifts that have been given to you.

2.**Make time for you.** This is a hard thing to do, but essential. I set the kids' bedtimes at 8:30 pm. After they are in the bed, I do a few chores and then I relax. I try to make sure that I leave myself time to wind down and think. Sometimes I read, sometimes I watch TV, sometimes I listen to music. Maybe at lunch instead of eating with your friends you can eat alone. In the morning before the kids get up, take some extra time to think and prepare for your day. Whatever relaxes you, leave yourself a little time during the day, even if it is just an hour.

3. **Pamper yourself.** About once a month, do something for yourself. If you have been throwing change in the piggy bank for a few months, dig some of that change out and get your nails done. Get a massage from your significant other, or, buy yourself that perfume that you have been wanting. Sometimes on Friday nights I buy the dessert that I really want but know that I do not need. Just make sure to do something for yourself once in a while.

List 2 activities that relax you, and a time during the day that you can fit these in.

This week I will relax by:
1. _____
   _____
2. _____
   _____

4. **Plan your life.** Almost everything in life is easier to execute when you have a plan. Take the time to make goals for yourself. Write out the steps that you will need to take to achieve the goals (see

the appendix on page 65). Be sure to choose realistic goals that challenge you, and reward yourself when the goal is met. After you achieve your goals, set new ones. It is important that parents are constantly growing and maturing. If you do not know where you are going then you need to figure it out and plan on how you will get there!

 5.**Exercise & get fit.** Your health influences all other aspects of your life. If you are in good shape, maintain it by exercising and eating right. If you are overweight or have a poor diet, work on improving yourself. The more in shape you are, the more energy that you have for work, your kids, and all the other activities that you want to pursue. A healthy diet will maintain your skin, organs, hair, and attitude.

 Eating healthy and exercising can be expensive. Fruit, vegetables, and salads are not cheap, so you need to plan your meals carefully and use the weekly sales papers to shop around for the best prices. If you cannot afford to join a gym to exercise try walking around your neighborhood or taking your kids to the park. If you have steps in your house, use them as a Stairmaster, or buy a jump rope and knock off a few pounds that way. Spring cleaning, yard work, and washing the car are also good ways of burning calories that can include the kids. When it comes to being healthy, do not make excuses. Make a way!

 6. **Improve your situation.** One of the best ways to feel better about yourself and your situation is to improve it. One of the blessings

associated with a struggle is the fact that when you do accomplish something you appreciate it more than you would have if it had been easy. Here are some things that you can do to improve your situation:

- **Vote.** When you vote, you ensure that your voice is being heard and you become empowered. Politicians will not care about the struggle of single parents if we are not the people that are voting them into office.
- **Move.** If you live in a high crime area or filthy conditions, save up your money and make a plan to move. Sometimes when you are in a destitute area you unknowingly become just like your surroundings.
- **Network.** Get out and get to know people. The more people that you know, the more people that you can call on when you need help.
- **Volunteer.** Volunteer work is a way of giving back to your community, helping others in need, and staying grounded. If you think that your situation is rough, take the time to help a person that has less than you and you will realize that things are not so bad.
- **Update your resume.** You should constantly update your resume, even if you are not actively looking for a new job. Once a year, get it professionally done. It may cost a little, but it will pay off when you have to use it.

y
IV. YOUR SPIRITUALITY

14. Getting Started

Attempting to take all of the steps in this book is a daunting task that is virtually impossible when attempted alone. To be successful you need a sound support system, whether it is your family, friends, or significant other. But even without those resources, you are still not alone. Your greatest strength and power will come from the spiritual relationship that you develop, nurture, and feed continuously throughout your life.

I tried and failed many times during my life to do things on my own. I wanted to be independent and prove that I was not a failure and that I could succeed without anyone's help. Attempting this feat caused me to put up my own stumbling blocks, which stalled my progress and created unnecessary stress in every aspect of my life. It took me banging my head against a wall for years and wondering why the world seemed to be against me for me to realize that the answers to all of my problems had been before me the entire time. I just had to open my eyes and look.

When I say I created my own stumbling blocks, it was not because I did not believe in God. I have always believed in God and knew that he existed and that Jesus died for my sins. My problem was that I was not convinced and had not learned that I did not have to fight the battles that I was fighting alone. I already had a solider in the fight, I was not using him. Once I realized that God could handle all of my issues, problems and situations, my stress eased, my obstacles moved out of the way, and I started achieving more than I ever dreamed was possible. In this part of the book I will attempt to encourage you to take an easier route than I did. Do not waste precious years fighting battles that are not yours. Turn all of your problems and your life over to God.

The hardest part of changing my life was getting started. I looked at getting closer to God and changing my ways as a huge, daunting task that I needed to do one day, but not right now. I could not imagine going to church EVERY Sunday, or going to bible study or Sunday school every week. I was not ready to talk to people that I did not know about God, or to stop enjoying my casual college life. I was not quite ready to change my friends and to stop gossiping about people and just live right in general. I was not a bad person, but I was not quite ready to be *that* good.

I made up wonderful excuses about why it was not time to get involved in church. When I was pregnant, I did not want to go because people would look at me and judge me for being a young single pregnant woman. After I had my daughter, I could not go because she was an infant and would cry in church and disrupt the service. When she was a toddler she would not sit still, so I could not go because those terrible two's were too much to handle for two hours. Next I had a part time job and my only morning to sleep was Sunday morning. I kept finding excuses and years went by and I still had not joined a church. Suddenly I was pregnant again after just graduating from college, and I was repeating a mistake that I had sworn never to make again.

List the 2 major things that are keeping you from strengthening your relationship with God.

I cannot change my life now because:
1. _____
   _____
2. _____
   _____

For me it took getting up one Sunday and going to a new church to truly change my life. It did not happen over night, or in a month, or even in a year. I learned in one sermon that if I took one step, God would take two. The more that I went to church and learned about the bible and learned about God, I learned that I was starting to change my view of my life and the things that I liked to do. The more that I surrounded myself with God, the more that I wanted to be around him. I went from dragging myself to church to jumping out bed in anticipation of going. I began to get my children involved in church activities, and suddenly I had to go to the church on Sunday to see them in the choir or to watch my daughter dance.

I learned how to let go of my past and my mistakes because God had already forgiven me, I just needed to forgive myself. I want to save you the trouble of living your life without God, but it is a decision that you have to make for yourself. Look back at your reasons, or excuses, for not getting closer to God. Are they really more important than your spiritual well being? Here are a few things that worked for me that will hopefully steer you in the right direction

1. **Read the bible for yourself.** I have heard many stories about the bible from friends, family members, pastors, and books. But if you were to ask me where the stories were in the bible, I would not have a clue. I had skimmed the passages before, but I never took the time to study the passages and learn them in context. If you asked me what conclusions I could draw from the stories, I could only repeat what I had heard others say because I had not read and understood it for myself. One way to truly understand God's love for you is to read the bible and learn about it for yourself.

Hearing the words, and actually reading them for yourself are two totally different experiences. I decided one day, after attending church for two years strong, that I wanted to sit down and read the bible. I started from Genesis, and am still in the process of reading it from beginning to end. Many times when I start reading, I have to make myself put it down. They say it is the greatest story ever told, but that is an understatement! I am learning from reading the bible that now I can come to my own conclusions and that I do not have to believe what I hear. If someone tells me something about God, they better be able to back it up because I am learning the truth for myself!

How much time did you spend watching TV today? _____
How much of this time are you willing to devote to reading the bible? _____.

2. **Find a good church**. It seems like it should be easy to find a church in this day and age because they are great in number. You should not, however, join the first church that you get to in the phone book. You need to take your time and visit different churches. Go with a coworker or friend, and find a church that fits you and your needs. When I was searching for a church I went to eight different ones over a six month period before I found one that I was comfortable with! Do you want to attend a large church or small? What denomination are you? Does the church have activities for your kids? What types of ministries are available? You should consider everything from whether or not they have more than one service to if

you enjoy the choir. This decision is major because this is going to be YOUR church. Take your time and make a wise decision.

3. **Find a mentor.** Young Christians need a mentor for many reasons. One is to have a person that you can talk to during your trying times. Just because you are changing your life does not mean that your problems will go away. It simply means that you are now equipped to deal with them. Often challenges are thrown at us that we do not know how to handle or are not sure how to approach. Having an older person in your life that can talk with you and pray with and for you is irreplaceable.

Another reason that young single parents need a mentor is because we can learn from them. Even though we may think that we have all of the answers, we often do not. A mentor can lead you in the right direction, and answer questions that you may not feel comfortable asking your parents, pastor, or even friends. A mentor is that extra boost of confidence, that person that whispers in your ear that everything will be all right. Take the time to find one for yourself and your children in your community.

Think of 2 people that may be able to serve as your spiritual mentors. If you do not know any, find one!

Two excellent mentors would be:

1. _____
2. _____

4. **Pray.** Praying is simply an intimate conversation with God. Many people are guilty of praying only when we are in trouble or in need. Think about how the entire country flocked to church after the terrorist attacks, or how we prayed for God's mercy during the Hurricane Katrina disaster. It is wonderful that we know to turn to God during trying times, but please take the time to pray when things are both bad and good. Pray for yourself and others around you. Pray for your children, your friends and family, and the world. Pray for forgiveness. Thank God in your prayers for your blessings. Pray for the things that you need and talk to God about what is bothering you. Even if you do not know how to pray, ask God to lead you and guide your heart. When I first realized that my relationship with God needed help, I prayed every night that God would strengthen my faith and lead me to him, and he did just that.

List 4 things that you are thankful for, 3 things that you need to repent for, and 2 things that you want God to bless you with.

I am thankful for:

1. _____
2. _____
3. _____
4. _____

I should repent for:

1. _____
2. _____
3. _____

I want God to bless me with:

1. _____
2. _____

Which list was easiest for you to come up with? Which was hardest? If you need more lines to list the blessings that you want from God, go back to page 52 and review the reasons that you are not ready to turn your life over to God. If you can get rid of these reasons, you can add to your blessings!

5. **Take your children to church**. Even if you are not ready to change your life, you owe your child the chance to get to know God. This world is cruel and attempting to enter it unarmed is dangerous. Allow your children the privilege and the honor of learning about God and how to model their lives after the bible. Even if you do not attend with them, let a grandparent or a friend take your children to Sunday School and church events. Do not punish your child because you are not ready for God. When they are older they will need the lessons that they learn in church for the rest of their lives.

List 2 activities that your children can become involved in at church. (Ex: Dance, choir, ushering, Sunday School, etc.)

My kids can become active in church by:

1. _____
   _____

2. _____
   _____

15. Change Your Life

One of the first and most important things that I learned on my journey is to trust God. I had to learn to pray for what I needed, whether it was for my bills to be paid, my grades, my safety, or my health, then turn it over to God. I was notorious for praying for something, then worrying about it. I learned in church that worrying is disbelief. There are things in your life that you need to learn and change. There are many things that young single parents need to accomplish while they are raising their children. The strength of God can help you do those things successfully, such as going back to college or making enough money to pay your bills. Go to church, figure out what your weaknesses are, and work on them. It is not as easy as it sounds, but God will continuously bless you with each step that you take. Major ways to change your life include:

- Surrounding yourself with God fearing people.
- Practicing what you preach.
- Teaching others what you have learned.
- Having faith and never giving up.
- Being thankful for what you have been given and not worrying about what you do not have.
- Continue to read the bible and other Christian literature.

List 2 major changes that you need to make in your life today. What is the first step in making these changes?

I need to change:
1. _____
    First Step: _____
    _____

2. _____
    First Step: _____
    _____

16. Talk About God

In the family that I grew up in we believed in God, we said our prayers at night, and we went to church on a fairly regular basis. We did not however, do some of the other essential things. We did not talk about God. We did not discuss how God could help us in our life. And we did not pray together. With your children, take the time to talk to them about what they are hearing and learning in church. Too often, children sit in church and listen to a sermon that is directed at adults. They hear what the preacher is saying, but they do not understand it, or they may not understand how it relates to them. Take the time to ask your children if they have questions. Read the bible with them and explain how different circumstances relate to them.

I remember as a teenager I was curious about sex, but I did not know how to fight my curiosity. I knew that I needed to protect myself because I would be in big trouble if I got pregnant, but I was unclear on why I should avoid sex altogether. I knew that the bible spoke against it, but why? What was so bad about it other than diseases and getting pregnant? If I had known the other consequences of premarital sex, such as the mental implications and why God truly does not want his children to engage in sexual misconduct, maybe I would have made better choices.

Try approaching your children's issues biblically. Tell them why they should obey their teacher, choose different friends, and avoid drugs and alcohol from God's perspective. Show them television programs and give them books that can help answer questions that you cannot. Also, pray with your children. As you learn how to pray, teach them how to pray as well. If you do these things with them at a young age, they will feel comfortable with these things as adults.

List 2 issues that your children have that should be approached through the bible:

My children's issues are:

1. _____
   _____

2. _____
   _____

CONCLUSIONS

Becoming a teenage parent or a young unwed mother is one of the toughest challenges out there. You are forced to grow up in a matter of months and the road that you will have to travel will not be an easy one. Many people will look down on you and judge you because of your mistakes. Nothing that you attempt to accomplish will be easy, and it will take everything that you have to raise your child in the healthy and prosperous environment that they deserve. It is so easy to give up or settle for less because of obstacles that you will face, but you owe it to yourself and your child not to take the easy way out. You can be successful. You can be happy and have a prosperous life. Making this choice which is going to affect the rest of your life does not have to be the beginning of the end.

After you overcome the trials that you are going to be faced with, you will be stronger and wiser. You will have strength that other women in their twenty's and thirty's have yet to muster up. Your children will admire your strength and learn from your mistakes and your guidance. Do not step aside and let life run over you. Further your education and pursue the career that you dreamed of having. Manage your finances and save money. Build strong relationships within your family and your community. Remember that you will only be alone in your journey if you choose to be. Take the initiative to build your support system and your relationship with God so that you have the power to triumph in every aspect of your life. With God, you and your children have the power to overcome the odds and ignore the statistics. Take the term single parent and give it a new meaning: Success.

APPENDIX

After completing this book, you should have an idea of the steps that you need to begin to take to change your life. Use the next few pages to compile all of the data that you have written down in this book. Use the answers that you have written to guide your steps, create goals, and monitor your progress. If you need to update or change your goals, do so.

List the 2 major goals that you want to accomplish in the next 6 months, your time-table for completing these goals, and your actual completion date. BE SPECIFIC! Your time-table should be in weeks or months. Do not set goals that are too easy or too farfetched. In chapter 14 you listed two things that you wanted God to bless you with (page 58). Incorporate these into your goals as well. Get your mentor to go over your goals with you to make sure that they are attainable and appropriate goals for your situation.

DATE: _____

GOAL #1: _____
_____
_____
_____
_____

MAJOR STEPS NEEDED TO COMPLETE:

1. _____
_____

2. _____
_____

3. _____
_____

TIME PERIOD: _____

CHAPTERS THAT YOU SHOULD REFERENCE: _____

COMMENTS (PARENT OR MENTOR):
_____
_____
_____

ACTUAL COMPLETION DATE: _____

DATE: _____

GOAL #2: _____

_____

_____

_____

_____

MAJOR STEPS NEEDED TO COMPLETE:

1. _____

2. _____

3. _____

TIME PERIOD: _____

CHAPTERS THAT YOU SHOULD REFERENCE: _____

COMMENTS (PARENT OR MENTOR):

_____

_____

_____

ACTUAL COMPLETION DATE: _____

DATE: _____

GOAL #3: _____

_____
_____
_____
_____

MAJOR STEPS NEEDED TO COMPLETE:

1. _____

2. _____

3. _____

TIME PERIOD: _____

CHAPTERS THAT YOU SHOULD REFERENCE: _____

COMMENTS (PARENT OR MENTOR):

_____
_____
_____

ACTUAL COMPLETION DATE: _____

Raising Your Child & Yourself

DATE: _____

GOAL #4: _____

_____

_____

_____

MAJOR STEPS NEEDED TO COMPLETE:

1. _____

_____

2. _____

_____

3. _____

_____

TIME PERIOD: _____

CHAPTERS THAT YOU SHOULD REFERENCE: _____

COMMENTS (PARENT OR MENTOR):

_____

_____

_____

ACTUAL COMPLETION DATE: _____

About the Author:

LaKeisha Giles was born in Milwaukee, WI, but grew up in the small town of Salisbury, NC. As a bright-eyed child, her wild imagination often got her into big trouble. Instead of always telling the truth, she would often dream up more fascinating accounts of events. As she grew older, she was regularly called upon to recant tales of events, which she did by adding vivid details to brighten the story. One day, she decided to try and brighten the stories of her life.

LaKeisha, who currently works for a non-profit organization and is pursing her MBA, graduated from college with a bachelor's degree in Computer Science (CS), and a minor in math. Although CS is not the ideal major for a writer, it was being told by a college professor that she spoiled the myth that mathematicians cannot write that encouraged her to pursue becoming a published writer. She writes short stories, fiction novels, and non-fiction. When she is not working, reading, playing sports, or spending time with her kids, she is in her hometown of Salisbury, working on that novel that will one day be published.

To learn more about the Author or obtain more copies of this book, please go to www.Lulu.com. You can also email her at: RochelleG52@Lycos.com.

www.ingramcontent.com/pod-product-compliance
Lightning Source LLC
Chambersburg PA
CBHW020020050426
42450CB00005B/572